The Bradshaw Movie Co

Compiled and written by
John Bradshaw and Robert DeMayo

Photos restored by
Sedona Photo Express

ISBN: 978-0-9833453-7-4
Wayward Publishing 2013

Edited by: Nina Rehfeld

Cover image: Bob Bradshaw dressed as the Lone Ranger for a commercial shoot.

Bob Bradshaw: Not your average photographer.

Bob often described himself as, "a simple man of few words with a deep appreciation for nature." Thanks to this collection we can share some of his unique experiences. He was one of the very first Marlboro Men, and he outlived most of the others because he didn't smoke. He was friends with Charles Bronson and rode through Monument Valley with him to visit his Navajo friends. He hung out with Elvis when they filmed Stay Away Joe on the Bradshaw Ranch. For years he was a principal photographer for Arizona Highways. He left his mark on Sedona.

Riders of the Purple Sage

1931 – 20th Century Fox – Directed by Hamilton MacFadden.
Starring George O'Brien.

Robber's Roost

1932 – Fox Films – Directed by Louis King and David Howard. Written by Zane Grey. Starring George O'Brien and Maureen O'Sullivan.

"Robber's Roost"

George O'Brien and Maureen O'Sullivan.

Note: Bell Rock in the background.

Texas Trail

1937 – Paramount Pictures – Directed by David Selman.
Starring William Boyd and George "Gabby" Hayes.

Billy the Kid

1941 – MGM – Directed by David Miller - Produced by Irving Asher.
Starring Robert Taylor and Brian Donlevy.

Note: Taken from Merry-Go-Round Rock with Bear Wallow Canyon in the background.

"Billy the Kid"

Robert Taylor and Brian Donlevy.

Last of the Duanes

1941 - 20th Century Fox – Directed by James Tinling - Produced by Sol Wurtzel.
Written by Zane Grey.
Starring George Montgomery and Lynne Roberts.

Tall in the Saddle

1944 – RKO Radio Pictures – Directed by Edwin L. Marin - Produced by Robert Fellows.
Starring John Wayne and Ella Raines.

*"This is the way West Sedona looked in the 1940's.
Filming could be done without a building in sight."* (Bob Bradshaw)

Angel and the Badman

1946 – Republic Pictures – Directed by James Edward Grant.
Produced by John Wayne Productions.
Starring John Wayne and Gail Russell.

Note: Courthouse Butte in the background.

"Angel and the Badman"

John Wayne and Gail Russell.

Note: Image taken on Merry-go-round Rock.

"Angel and the Badman"

John Wayne and Gail Russell.

"Angel and the Badman"

Note: Taken from Boynton Pass with the base of Bear Mountain in the background.

California

1946 – Paramount Pictures –Directed by John Farrow.
Produced by Seton Miller and John Farrow.
Starring Ray Milland and Barbara Stanwyck.

16   *Note: The following page shows wagons being lowered near Merry-Go-Round Rock.*

Desert Fury

1947 – Paramount Pictures – Directed by Lewis Allen - Produced by Hal Wallis.
Starring Elizabeth Scott, John Hodiak and Burt Lancaster.

Note: Overlooking the Cowpies, off Schnebly Hill Road.

Cheyenne

1947 – Warner Brothers – Directed by Raoul Walsh.
Starring Dennis Morgan and Jane Wyman.

Note: Picture taken at today´s location of the Chapel of the Holy Cross.

Gunfighters

1947 – Columbia Pictures – Directed by George Waggner - Produced by Harry Joe Brown. Starring Randolph Scott, Barbara Britton and Dorothy Hart.

Note: This film is an adaption of Zane Grey's novel "Twin Sombreros".

Albuquerque

1948 - Paramount Pictures – Directed by Ray Enright.
Starring Randolph Scott and Barbara Britton.

The Fabulous Texan

1948 – Republic Pictures – Directed by Edward Ludwig.
Starring William Elliott, John Carroll and Catherine McLeod.

"The Fabulous Texan"

William Elliot and Catherine McLeod.

Station West

1948 – RKO Radio Pictures – Directed by Sidney Lanfield - Produced by Robert Sparks. Starring Dick Powell, Jane Greer, Agnes Moorehead, and Burl Ives.

"Station West"

Dick Powell and Jane Greer.

Blood on the Moon

1948 – RKO Radio Pictures – Directed by Robert Wise – Produced by Theron Warth.
Starring Robert Mitchum, Barbara Bel Geddes and Robert Preston.

Note: This image was taken at Red Rock Crossing.

"Blood on the Moon"

Robert Mitchum and Barbara Bel Geddes.

The Strawberry Roan

1948 – Columbia Pictures – Directed by John English – Produced by Armand Schaefer.
Starring Gene Autry, Gloria Henry, and Jack Holt.

"The Strawberry Roan"

Note: Chapel area.

Next page: The horse standing on the block is Champion. Over Gene Autry's career, his horse became so popular he got his own TV series. This image was taken at Merry-Go-Round Rock.

Coroner Creek

1948 – Columbia Pictures – Produced by Harry Joe Brown – Directed by Ray Enright.
Starring Randolph Scott and Marguerite Chapman.

Hellfire

1949 – Republic Pictures – Directed by Robert G. Springsteen.
Starring Wild Bill Elliot, Marie Windsor, Jim Davis, Forrest Tucker, and Paul Fix.

Comanche Territory

1950 – Universal Pictures – Directed by George Sherman – Produced by Leonard Goldstein. Starring Maureen O'Hara and Carey Macdonald.

Note: Red Rock loop with Cathedral Rock in the background.

"Comanche Territory"

Ernest Borgnine on the left.

Copper Canyon

1950 – Paramount Pictures – Directed by John Farrow – Produced by Mel Epstein.
Starring Ray Milland and Hedy Lamarr.

Note: Riders coming out of Bear Wallow Canyon with the Cowpies behind them.

"Copper Canyon"

*Note: Location – Red Rock Crossing. This building was erected and dismantled
by Bob Bradshaw for the film. Part of his fee was that he kept the lumber,
which he used to build Sedona's first photo shop, one of the first Kodak
shops in the Southwest. Rollies Camera Shop now operates in this building.*

The Eagle and the Hawk

1950 – Paramount Pictures – Directed by Lewis R. Foster.
Produced by William H. Pine and William C. Thomas.
Starring John Payne, Rhonda Fleming and Dennis O'Keefe.

"The Eagle and the Hawk"

Note: This film was originally released as "Spread Eagle".

Broken Arrow

1950 - 20th Century Fox Film – Directed by Delmer Daves.
Produced by Julian Blaustein.
Starring James Stewart, Jeff Chandler and Debra Paget.

"Broken Arrow"

James Stewart and Debra Paget.

"Broken Arrow"

James Stewart (left) and Jeff Chandler (right).

"Broken Arrow"

"I worked as a carpenter on "Broken Arrow" while my wife, Bea, ran our little photo supply store. The Hollywood carpenter boss, Paul Wurtzel, liked me and gave me several truckloads of lumber that were left over from the set construction. I transported them over to the four acres I bought in Little Horse Park up where the Chapel of the Holy Cross is now." (Bob Bradshaw)

Red Head and the Cowboy

1951 – Paramount Pictures – Directed by Leslie Fenton – Produced by Irving Asher.
Starring Glenn Ford, Rhonda Fleming and Edmond O'Brien.

Red Head and the Cowboy

Note: This scene was shot in West Sedona near Posse Grounds.

"For 'The Redhead and the Cowboy' we also built a barn on the Woo Ranch and fixed up the old frame house with gun ports and shuttered windows." (Bob Bradshaw)

Indian Uprising

1952 – Columbia Pictures – Directed by Ray Nazzaro – Produced by Bernard Small.
Starring George Montgomery and Audrey Long.

Note: Courthouse Butte and Bell Rock in the distance.

"Indian Uprising"

*Note: This was one of the first Westerns that recognized the Native Americans´
case: White people (miners in this film) were trespassing on their land
and breaking treaties.*

Singing Guns

1951 – Republic Pictures – Directed by Robert G. Springsteen.
Starring Vaughn Monroe, Ella Raines, Walter Brennan and Ward Bond.

Note: The Location is the Chapel area with Cathedral Rock in the background.

Flamming Feather

Half Breed

1952 – RKO Radio Pictures– Directed by Stuart Gilmore – Produced by Herman Schlom.
Starring Robert Young, Janis Carter, and Jack Buetel.

Note: This was shot just below Cathedral Rock.

"Half Breed"

*"I worked on `The Half-Breed´ in 1952 as an actor in the cavalry.
On the same movie, I also got the job as both a double and a
stand-in for Robert Young."*

(Bob Bradshaw)

Pony Soldier

1952 – 20th Century Fox Film – Directed by Joseph M. Newman.
Produced by Samuel Engel.
Starring Tyrone Power, Thomas Gomez, Robert Horton and Penny Edwards.

Note: Location – Red Rock Crossing with Cathedral Rock in the background.

"Pony Soldier"

Note: Sugarloaf Rock in West Sedona in background.

The two following pages have images from Pony Soldier.

Flaming Feather

1952 – Paramount Pictures – Directed by Ray Enright – Produced by Nat Holt.
Starring Sterling Hayden, Barbara Rush, Victor Jory,
Forrest Tucker, Arleen Whelan, and Edgar Buchanan.

56 *Note: Several pages back, soldiers attacking Montezuma's Castle (from this film).*

Gun Fury

1953 – Columbia Pictures – Directed by Raoul Walsh – Produced by Lewis Rachmil. Starring Rock Hudson, Donna Reed, Phil Carey, Roberta Haynes and Lee Marvin.

Note: Cathedral Rock in the background.

"Gun Fury"

*"I was part of the crew that built the original set under Coffee Pot Rock,
which was used for many movies until it was torn down in 1960."*
(Bob Bradshaw)

Gun Fury

"In 1953, I worked on 'Gun Fury' and doubled for both Rock Hudson and Lee Marvin."
(Bob Bradshaw)

Johnny Guitar

1954 – Republic Pictures - Directed by Nicholas Ray.
Starring Joan Crawford, Sterling Hayden, Mercedes McCambridge, Scott Brady,
Ward Bond, Ernest Borgnine, John Carradine, Ben Cooper, Royal Dano.

Note: Bob Bradshaw was an extra in this film.

Johnny Guitar

"`Johnny Guitar´ was also made that year and I rode through most of the picture with Ward Bond. We were the men in black suits that he rounded up out of the funeral scene to chase Scott Brady, Ernest Borgnine, and the rest of the bad men."

(Bob Bradshaw)   61

Apache

1954 - United Artists – Directed by Robert Aldrich – Produced by Harold Hecht.
Starring Burt Lancaster, Jean Peters, John McIntyre and Charles Buchinsky.

Note: Bob Bradshaw worked as a mounted Indian scout in this film.

The Outlaw's Daughter

1954 – 20th Century Fox – Directed and produced by Wesley Barry.
Starring Bill Williams, Kelly Ryan, and Jim Davis.

Drum Beat

1954 – Warner Brothers Pictures - Directed and produced by Delmer Daves.
Starring Alan Ladd, Audrey Dalton, Charles Bronson and Marisa Pavan.

Note: Cathedral Rock in the distance.

"Drum Beat"

"I worked as a cavalry soldier on `Drum Beat´. Charles Buchinsky was our leader in this script. He later changed his last name to Bronson." (Bob Bradshaw)

Note: Chimney Rock in the distance.

Stranger on Horseback

1955 – United Artists – Directed by Jacques Tourneur – Produced by Robert Goldstein.
Original Story by Louis L'Amour.
Starring Joel McCrea, Miroslava, and John McIntire.

"*Stranger on Horseback*"

"*I did a lot of horseback riding for stars when it was too dangerous or
when they were just not skilled enough to ride.*" (Bob Bradshaw)

Note: Bell Rock in the distance.

Shotgun

1955 – Allied Artists – Directed by Lesley Selander - Produced by John C. Champion. Starring Sterling Hayden, Zachary Scott, and Yvonne DeCarlo.

Shotgun

"I worked as a stand-in and double for Zachary Scott on `Shotgun´ in 1955."
(Bob Bradshaw)

Note: The images on the next two pages are from "Shotgun".

The Last Wagon

1956 – 20th Century Fox – Directed by Delmer Daves – Produced by William Hawks.
Starring Richard Widmark and Felicia Farr.

Note: This scene shot near Merry-Go-Round Rock.

"The Last Wagon"

"I worked on the `Last Wagon´ as a double for Timothy Carey, who was one of the bad-men."

(Bob Bradshaw)

"The Last Wagon"

Note: This scene was filmed in Bear Wallow Canyon just above the Cowpies.

3:10 to Yuma

1957 - Columbia Pictures - Directed by Delmer Daves – Produced by David Heilweil.
Starring Glenn Ford, Van Heflin, and Felicia Farr.

"3:10 to Yuma"

Glenn Ford.

Note: Bob Bradshaw was an extra in this film.

Yellowstone Kelly

1959 – Warner Brothers Pictures – Directed by Gordon Douglas.
Starring Clint Walker, Ed Byrnes, John Russell and Andrea Martin.

"I worked on `Yellowstone Kelly´ as a cavalry soldier. We started in Flagstaff with 165 soldiers and they sent 20 of us to Sedona to have a war with the Indians." (Bob Bradshaw)

The Legend of Lobo

1962 – Walt Disney.

"I scouted locations for this film and a lot of scenes were filmed around the Bradshaw Ranch and the Indian ruins in Red Canyon. The company had two wolves for most of the close-ups and 45 wolves were kept at the ranch." (Bob Bradshaw)

The Rounders

1965 – MGM – Directed by Burt Kennedy – Produced by Dick Lyons.
Starring Glenn Ford, Henry Fonda, Chill Wills, Sue Anne Langdon, and Hope Holiday.

Stay Away Joe

1968 - MGM– Directed by Peter Tewksbury – Produced by Doug Laurence.
Starring Elvis Presley, Katy Jurado, Burgess Meredith, Joan Blondell, L.Q. Jones, Warren Vanders, Buck Kartalian, Susan Trustman, Quentin Dean, Henry Jones, Anne Seymour, Thomas Gomez, Doug Henderson, Angus Duncan, and Michael Lane.

Stay Away Joe

Note: These images, and the one on the next page, were all taken at the Bradshaw Ranch.

"When Elvis was in town, the red rocks were buzzing with electricity. I found a house for him to stay in below King's Ransom Hotel. I found another place for his Memphis Mafia. Elvis was a nice guy, very down to earth." (Bob Bradshaw)

Stay Away Joe

The Legend of the Eagle and the Boy

1968 – Walt Disney – Written and Directed by Jack Couffer.
Starring Frank DeKova and Stanford Lomakema.

The Wild Rovers

1971 – MGM – Directed by Black Edwards – Produced by Ken Wales.
Starring William Holden, Ryan O'Neal, Karl Malden,
Tom Skerritt, Joe Don Baker, and Victor French.

Note: Filmed on the Bradshaw Ranch.

Ace Ranchero

Note: Bob Bradshaw drawing his gun.

The next image is also from Ace Ranchero.

26 Men

1957 – ABC Television. Starring Kelo Henderson and Tristram Coffin.

"My first job as a coordinator, or contact man as they called us back then, was in 1956, securing the wagons and horses for the '26 Men' television series. I also worked as one of the 26 Arizona Rangers and did some of the stunts. In this image a stagecoach passes the base of Bell Rock. This 4-horse team belonged to me at the time." (Bob Bradshaw)

Wagons Westward

1976 - Filmed on the Bradshaw Ranch and Hart Prairie, Flagstaff.

"I furnished the three wagons and the canvas covers. My friend, J.D. Pritchard supplied the horse teams, and I used my good horse, Hosteen, to lead the wagons." (Bob Bradshaw)

"Wagons Westward"

*For this TV movie Bob Bradshaw played the part of the wagon master.
In this image, Bob is on the left with the white shirt and cowboy hot.*

Wagons Westward

"We did a lot of filming for television around Sedona, but no one had a TV set in town. We had to go to Cottonwood to view what we had filmed." (Bob Bradshaw)

Wagons Westward

Note: This scene was filmed in northern Arizona between Page and Tuba City.

John Bradshaw

John Bradshaw was ushered into this world like a true cowboy - his father Bob senior paid for his delivery with a colt. John began leading horseback tours at the age of nine, and by twelve, he was taking folks out by himself. In the mid-1990s John took over the Bradshaw Ranch as a destination for horseback rides and jeep tours. Over the years, the Bradshaw Ranch served as location for five movies, two TV series, and numerous commercials. John also purchased Sedona Photo Tours, a Forest Service Permitted company (now A Day in the West).

Sedona's First Tour Guides

When Don Pratt began giving jeep tours, Bob Bradshaw had been offering Sedona horseback rides for ten years. Don was a realtor and offered the tours for $3 to show people the land he had for sale. He created the Broken Arrow trail over one of Bob Bradshaw's horseback trails. One of Sedona's first jeep tour guides was Bob Bradshaw's son, Bob Bradshaw, Jr. Eventually Don sold the company, and three more owners would hold it before in 1988 the current owner, Shawn Wendell.

Bob Bradshaw (1918 – 2008)

Bob Bradshaw bought his first camera in 1939 and took photos for the next seven decades. He traveled all over the United States, but eventually chose the red rocks of Sedona as his primary motif. When he arrived in 1945 Sedona was a town of 300. Bob opened one of the first Kodak dealerships in Uptown Sedona just as the movie industry was taking off. He found work as a carpenter, stuntman, location scout, actor and wrangler. He also started the first trail rides in Sedona, departing from uptown.

BRADSHAW GALLERY

Keep a lookout for other Bradshaw books!

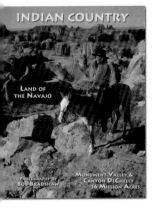 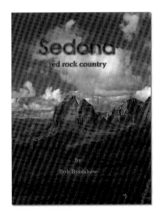  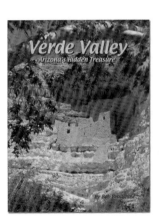 

Indian Country   **Sedona Red Rock country**   **Bob Bradshaw The Sedona Man**   **Verde Valley**   **Amazing Arizona**

For 75 years the Bradshaw Family has been showing visitors the best of Sedona. Help us continue...

A Day in the West
252 N. Hwy 89a
Sedona, AZ 86336

(928) 282-4320

www.adayinthewest.com
reserve@adayinthewest.com

Sedona Photo Express
150 Hwy 179, #9
Sedona, AZ 86336

(928) 282-6606

www.sedonaphoto.net
info@sedonaphoto.net

Bradshaw Color Studios
PO Box 1019
Sedona, AZ 86336

(928) 282-3131

www.bradshawgallery.com
jbradshaw@adayinthewest.com